Plant Biotechnology Education Programmes

Plant Biotechnology Education Programmes

From School to University

Wagdy A. Sawahel

Genetic Engineering & Biotechnology Division
National Research Centre, Cairo, Egypt

2024

Daya Publishing House®

A Division of

Astral International Pvt. Ltd.

New Delhi – 110 002

First Published, 1997
Reprinted, 2024

ISBN: 9788170351740 (PB)

Published by : **Daya Publishing House®**
A Division of
Astral International Pvt. Ltd.
– ISO 9001:2015 Certified Company
4736/23, Ansari Road, Darya Ganj
New Delhi-110 002
Ph. 011-43549197, 23278134
E-mail: info@astralint.com
Website: www.astralint.com

To my wife, L. Warner, for all her help and encouragement and especially for rescuing me on several occasions with the right word or turn of phrase.
To my daughter, Sarah, for whose generation I have written this book.

Acknowledgements

I wish to express my appreciation to many colleagues from various institutions, departments and countries all over the world who have provided me with valuable first-hand information, research finding and various forms of assistance. Notable among these are the following : Paul Wymer, Head of Communication and Education Department, The Wellcome Trust, London, UK; David Micklos, Director of DNA Learning Centre, New York, USA; BSCS (Biological Sciences Curriculum Study) Educational Research and Development Organization, Colorado College, USA; and Association for Science Education, Hatifield, UK.

This monograph was written during the tenure of research fellowship awarded to the author by the United Nations Industrial Development Organisation (UNIDO) and International Centre for Genetic Engineering and Biotechnology (ICGEB), which is hereby gratefully acknowledged.

Preface

Genetic Engineering and biotechnology are the latest in a series of technological innovations that have revolutionized the field of agriculture and the health sciences. Already great strides have been made in applying the techniques of molecular biology and genetic engineering to the problems of disease diagnosis, gene therapy and the development of new pharmaceuticals. In the agricultural industry this technology is being used to address many of the problems associated with the production of food and fibre.

Although biotechnology holds great promise for the agricultural and medical sciences, there is concern about the risks, both real and imagined, posed by this technology. For example, two-thirds of the American public are of the opinion that genetically altered bacteria represent a threat to the environment and nearly 50 per cent see a similar risk from genetically altered plants and animals. There are also ethical questions to be considered. Public opinion polls repeatedly find that a significant minority of Americans simple believe that genetic manipulation of plants and animals is morally wrong.

These many questions and concerns highlight the necessity of developing a significant dialogue among all the parties involved. Such a dialogue should include an emphasis on education and the development of an understanding of the principals involved in biotechnology research, product development and risk analysis. Only in this context can an interested public work hand-in-hand with industry officials, government regulators and environmental activists in making informed decisions about the development and regulation of this important industry.

To this end, it is the scientists role to create their own vital presence in the biotechnology education process. "Who would do it if not us scientists and who can do it better than a practising scientist? Scientists are members of society, and the fruits of their work under pin and shape it. Society requires and deserves that we enter into dialogue with it; communicating our science is an important as creating it." What we need is proper, regular, frequent, informed and discerning communication and education programmes of science. And the need is even more acute now in the era of genetic engineering. It is important and necessary to convince private industry and people and at large that long-term investment in genetic engineering research, development and education is vital for material welfare and national ethos*".

In writing this book, I have tried to draw together all the available information of plant genetic engineering, including whenever possible, all the most up-to-date technologies. In doing so I have aimed to achieving two goals. First of all, I have attempted to document the whole of this exciting area of research in order to describe what has been achieved so far, where the limitations lie, and what might still be achieved in the future. Secondly, I have tried to produce a basis book for plant genetic engineering education to provide teachers, lecturers, environmental activists, governmental regulators, industrial representatives and the public with a very well-planned programmes for education and training.

Finally, I sincerely hope that this book provides the reader a comprehensive education programmes for plant genetic engineering. I have tried to the best of my ability, to give credit to whom their work deserve recognition in this field.

8 December, 1996 WAGDY A. SAWAHEL

---

* The above quot is from Professor Peter Day, Director, the Royal Institutions, London, U.K., who delievered the Ninth Blackett Memorial Lecture of the Indian National Science Academy on 10 January 1994 (See *Current Science*, 1994, 67 : 434–440).

Contents

Introduction

Biotechnology has been hailed as the technological revolution of the end of the 20th century. It has raised hopes for accelerating economic advancement and the alleviation of hunger and disease in developing countries. Biotechnology was recently defined as "any technique that uses living organisms (or parts of living organisms) to make or modify products, or to improve plants or animals, for beneficial use." This broad definition covers recombinant DNA techniques, monoclonal antibodies, and so on. It can also be loosely constructed to include such traditional processes as the production of antibiotics and food processing by fermentation.

From the plant scientists point of view, agricultural and horticultural advantages are central to the perceived blessings of advances in plant genetic engineering and biotechnology. Twenty-five years ago the plant breeder wishing to produce a new variety was faced with the laborious and very random business of selecting plants over several generations. A decade ago the infant science of gene technology swept him off his feet, and released him from the drudgery of the greenhouse bench, converting him into a laboratory scientist, who not only nurtures genetic variation, but also fashions it. His products are increasingly designer, made-to-order, transgenic plants.

Recent advances in plant genetic engineering have created unprecedented opportunities for the genetic manipulation of plants. In addition, its potential impact on the genetic improvement of crop plants has generated considerable interest, enthusiasm, and optimism in the scientific community and is in part responsible for the rapidly expanding plant biotechnology industry. It does appear, however, that education programmes for plant genetic engineering, especially at high-school and undergraduate levels, have not advanced as plant genetic engineering research has done.

Plant biotechnology and genetic engineering are knowledge intensive areas of study. Biotechnology is small sale in terms of volumes and very labour-intensive, requiring an extremely skilled work force. Basic skills in the use of sophisticated instrumentation and techniques are, thus, central to the economics of plant biotechnology industry. Lack of rigorously trained manpower with hands-on experience can destroy a programme as effectively as lack of material resources. These basic skill are essentially the same for a career in industry or in the basic sciences.

Plant genetic engineering industry is bound to fail in the absence of scientific rigor. There is, therefore, a very definitive market for biotechnology education that integrates scientific rigor into the curriculum with the aim to provide industry with a highly-skilled manpower.

The book, therefore, includes information about planning of plant genetic engineering education system from high-school to post-graduate levels, syllabus design, course contents and teaching approaches.

The book provide biotechnology educationalists, policy-makers, researcher, teachers and lecturers with solutions for a lot of questions and problems such as how can modern plant biotechnology be integrated with conventional biology courses? Which priority problems can be addressed by biotechnology? Which technologies are relevant and accessible, and what will be the likely cost and impact? In addition, when learning about biotechnology, students often fail to grasp the scientific concept being taught because they are not fully aware of the forms of the DNA molecules, cells and processes involved. The book, therefore, provides useful teaching approaches that simplify the scientific concept which is being described. Furthermore, biotechnology research and applications have been very much in the public domain since the technology entered its "modern" phase in the 1970s. In the absence of the scientific voice and the disproportionate amount of media attention it has received, the public has developed a negative image of biotechnological activities. The book, therefore, focuses on scientific strategies for improving the public understanding of biotechnology, i.e., educating the public. Finally, the book provides a coherent and accurate account of the history of biotechnology and technical advances. This, is turn, will enhance biotechnology teaching and makes it come alive in the classroom; give warning about errors or past abuses we do not wish to see repeated; add to our world view; and stimulate insights into the process of discovery.

I. BIOTECHNOLOGY IN SCHOOLS

"The students are alive, and the purpose of education is to stimulate and guide self-development." A.N. Whitehead.

Human life is now permeated with sciences and civilization rests upon scientific foundations. The sciences are the greatest educational forces in generating true freedom of the mind, and thus must in fact constitute the heart of truly liberal education.

Molecular biology and biotechnology exemplify the new biology—the science of recombinant DNA, monoclonal antibodies, the human genome projects, bioenergetics and DNA probes, for example. These recent advances in biological research are revolutionizing classroom education because biotechnology affect all aspects of our lives and the lives of other organisms.

Generally speaking, the idea of biotechnology education depends in large part on working scientists, and especially on scientist-teacher partnerships, to create new classroom activities and curricula. These activities open the door for a more extensive examination of the principles of genetics and the moral, ethical, and legal issues that arise from new knowledge and technology in genetics.

To a great extent, public education will determine whether biotechnology is used to its fullest potential for personal health management or is misunderstood and feared. Clearly, society can not tolerate another era of abuse of the principles of genetics, such as occurred during the Nazi quest for racial purity.

If we believe in the Madisonian concept of an informed citizenry that participates in public decision making, then biotechnology literacy must become common place. Young people entering the medical, agricultural, manufacturing, and many other professions will be expected to have a basic command of biotechnology (Micklos, 1990). Much work has been begun but a great deal more remains to be undertaken, and the scientific community can make a significant contribution.

1. Genetic Literacy

The revolution in biotechnology is an important landmark in the science of biology (Table 1.1) (Bud, 1993 a, b), and new industry has emerged that has enabled scientists to have a greater understanding of the genetic structure of living organisms (Olsen, 1986).

The idea of moving genes about, while having breathtaking implication, has been quite disturbing. Much of the concern centres on philosophical, social, environmental, and ethical issues. Arguments range from those having the goal of enhancing the quality of life to those which raise the spectra of Hitlerian eugenics leading to the ultimate use of political mastery over its citizens (Boone, 1984).

Table 1.1 : The History of Biotechnology

Period	*Events*
A century ago–1895	* The transition stage in fermentation from craft roots to modern industry.
Seventy-seven years ago–1918	* The appearance of the word "Bio-tehnologie" in German.
	* Economic microbiology has come of age.
Sixty-two years ago–1933	* The first science fiction story about genetic engineering (Aldous Huxley's Brave New World)
Fifty-seven years ago–1938	* The beginning of structural biology with the X-ray crystallography of two classes of biological macromolecules (Protein & DNA)

Period	*Events*
	* The low-resolution determination reveals DNA as an organized structure, the "pile of pennies".
	* The appearance of the phrase "molecular biology".
Fifty-two years ago–1943	* Mass production of penicillin by an aerobic fermentation.
	* "Geneone enzyme" hypothesis which links bio-chemistry with genetics.
	* The beginning of bacterial genetics.
Forty-seven years ago–1948	* The first genetic map of bacteriophage.
	* The appearance of two phrases: chemical engineering and molecular medicine.
Forty-two years ago–1953	* The double helix structure of DNA was elucidated and molecular biology becomes the basis for understanding of life.
	* The fermentation route to cortisone provided a new boost for industrial microbiology.
Thirty-seven years ago–1958	* DNA polymerase discovered and its action demonstrated.
	* The first sequence of protein : insulin.
Thirty-two years ago–1963	* The discovery of restriction enzymes.
	* The development of solid phase peptide synthesis.
Twenty-seven years ago–1968	* The biological time bomb was published by a British Journalist, warning the public of potential impact of modern biology.
Twenty-two years ago–1973	* The process of recombining DNA *in vitro* was published and the age of the new biotechnology was born.

Period	Events
	* The discovery of monoclonal anti-bodies.
Seventeen years ago–1978	* The production of human insulin in *E. coli.*
	* The discovery of ways for DNA sequencing.
Twelve years ago–1983	* The first successful transfer of foreign DNA into plants using Ti-plasmid.
	* Plant molecular genetics has finally come of age.
Seven-years ago–1988	* "onco-mouse" the first mammal to be patented.
	* The first commercial PCR had been introduced.
	* The human genome project started.
Now–1996	* Things are moving so fast in biotech-nology that between the writing and the reading the world may have changed.
	* GATT talks about the world-wide agreement on regulation of biotech-nology products.
	* The establishment of the first com-pany to explore methods to replace and repair defective genes (genetic therapy)
	* DNA fingerprints had been accepted by USA law enforcement agencies as one of the most definitive evidence of identity in rape, murder, and paternity cases.

This unusual situation, in which the social implications of biotechnology were examined even before the technology was implemented, resulted in part from strong division within the scientific community over its environmental application. While contained biotechnology production is appropriate, the long-term environmental risks posed by biotechnology applied in the field are such that (the complex ecology of Earth may soon be transformed into an industrial "biosystem", with potentially catastrophic consequences) (Johnson, 1993). In fact, their is a need for this despoiled planet, to return more land to nature, and to facilitate the preservation of rare and endangered species. This indicates that biotechnology, if used appropriately, could be a tool for adding the conservation of genetic diversity, the bioremediation of damaged environments and for helping reduce the use of chemical fertilizers and pesticides (Fox, 1992).

Many of the arguments, or at least the response to such arguments, are emotional in nature and reflect the lack of knowledge concerning the underlying genetic engineering technology. It is all too easy, in the lack of real understanding of the issues, to form an opinion based on emotional rather than rational judgements.

In general, the public do not have the knowledge, nor the access to it, to be fully informed (Ingram, 1992). In 1987 Office of Technology Assessment Survey found that 63 per cent of Americans claim to have heard or read relatively little or almost nothing about "genetic engineering" and about 44 per cent can not give meaningful definition of the word. The National Science Foundation sponsored studies showed that only 10 per cent of the American public can explain what a molecule is, and only 22 per cent can define DNA correctly. A widely quoted set of surveys conducted by the National Science foundation indicated that a scant 7 per cent of US citizens are scientifically literate-in command of a basic vocabulary and grammar of scientific terms and concepts. A subsequent poll undertaken by the National Institute of Health to learn public knowledge of biomedical science reveals that the majority of those queried have very vague notions about the definitions of such fundamental terms as DNA and bacteria (Hassler, 1994).

As genetic engineering and molecular biology continue to move out of the laboratory into the public area in the form of drugs, therapies and food products, public education in biotechnology will be essential to the public assessment, and one would hope, public acceptance of the fruits of biotechnology's labour.

Against this background, increased genetic engineering literacy must be the joint aim of governments, industry and research science. The aim of increased biotechnology literacy can be pursued on many levels but sharing our science with young people at schools surely must be a central thrust in this campaign.

Technological literacy is, on the one hand, necessary to the foundation of skills for living a humane and productive life in a technological society. Technical literacy, however, extend beyond simply gaining an armamentarium of employable skills. More importantly, it refers to an education process that "prepare a citizenry to soundly evaluate biotechnological decisions which involved environmental risks and safety concerns, ethical issues, and full disclosure by private industry about the products (organisms) they have constructed" (Fiksel and Covello, 1986). As new technologies outdate existing laws, more appropriate regulations will be promulgated only to the degree that informed citizenry will give its assent.

Literacy, with respect to technology, can be summarized by an old Chinese proverb which says :

"Tell me and I will forget.

Show me and I might remember.

Involve me and I will understand."

And what better way to become involved in genetic engineering technology than to have students, early in their academic careers, embrace some of the simpler procedures and techniques that result in the transfer of genes between microorganisms. From such modest beginers come the future scientists who may discover new strategies for cancer prevention, develop the ability to correct genetic abnormalities using cloned genes, or construct microorganisms which might produce new and better compounds effective in the treatment of cardiovascular disease. Equally important, however, will be the potential for generating an informed public, one that raises questions based upon insight and knowledge rather than succumbs to the emotional dictates of those who rely upon ignorance (Thomas, 1988). In addition, the appreciation of the applicability of genetic engineering technology to the physician and researcher, as well as its profound, potential effects on society. Furthermore, the student's recognition that he and/or she must assume responsibility for assuring that such effects are used for the betterment of mankind (Dixon, 1988).

2. Biotechnology Education Programme

Today's students will live their adult lives in an era influenced significantly by rapid advances in science and technology.

Probably no area of science is more important, or has advanced further in the lat years than genetics, supported by increased knowledge of molecular biology, cell biology, and biochemistry. The most recent scientific excitement has developed from significant advances in biotechnology and genetic engineering.

A well-defined plan, including objectives, strategies, and teaching approaches, is needed to help move biotechnology education into the next century and address the contemporary issues of updating science content, incorporating new pedagogies and implementing new programmes. The content of biotechnology courses should focus less on the recall and verification of trivial information and terms, and concentrate more on the development of conceptual schemes and the unifying principles of biotechnology.

A. Programme's Objectives

Biotechnology knowledge must be placed in its fullest perspective. The students should acquire not only an intellectual and esthetic appreciation for the complexities of living things and their interrelationships in nature, but also for ways in which the new knowledge is gained and tested, old errors eliminated, and an ever closer approximation to truth attained (Glass, 1993).

The programme should fulfill the following important objectives, which essential parallel student development :

* to acquaint students with basic biology of genetic engineering and the use of biotechnology to study basic problems in genetics, evolution, and health care.
* to inculcate basic tenets of genetic literacy.
* to promote an appreciation for the personal and societal problems generated by genetic engineering.
* to introduce the students to ethical analysis and the formation of public policy with respect to gene technology.
* to encourage the use of a scientific method for problem solving and critical thinking and to help students develop those skills.
* to encourage students to think about issues in research technology, public policy, discoveries and careers.

B. Programme's Strategies

The programme should provide the following strategies (Glass, 1993) that address the need to provide a biotechnology education for all students :

* cooperative learning;

* experiences that encourage the development of spatial skills and skills in cognitive processing;
* introduction to careers in biotechnology;
* topics that are relevant to the student's lives and activities that build on prior experiences of all students;
* activities that promote critical thinking;
* skills that will increase the student's chances of success in school;
* language and artwork that reflect a balanced representation of gender, race, and physical capabilities; and
* textbook contains current and informative articles, stories, editorials, letters and interviews presented in a format that is interesting and popular with students.

C. Programme's Outline

The development of biotechnology curricula at all levels (elementary, middle and high schools) should involve scientists, teachers, and educators. The knowledge imparts should not only be important in itself but also promotes values of personal autonomy and public participation.

It has been reported that there is growing awareness among educators that a basic understanding of genetics, disease risk, and health choices is an essential element of cultural literacy—as important in the education of developing child as is a basic understanding of hygiene and nutrition (Micklos, 1992).

Against the above requirements, the biotechnology curricula should include the following :

* Traditional (old) biotechnology.

* Genetics in history (Gregory Mendel).
* Genetic resources.
* The DNA molecule.
* Tools of genetic engineer.
* Recent advances in biotechnology (e.g. Gene therapy, DNA fingerprint, Genetic testing).
* Ethical social, environmental, legal and safety issues.

3. Biotechnology Teaching Approaches

The manner in which science is taught causes young people to become so disinterested in science. The students spend preponderance of the class time listening to teacher's lectures and only have few opportunities to explore natural phenomena directly or engage in discussions about the limited experiences that they did have. The scientific content in these classes appears to be largely textbook and/or word-book-driven, reflecting little, or not at all, the recent biotechnological advances. Hand-on laboratories are the exception, rote memorization is the norm (Micklos et. al., 1989).

A. Model Construction Approach

In teaching abstract concepts it is often useful to provide some form of visualization which enables students to "see" the concept which is being described. Models of various structures can be used to great effect, and may help those students who have difficulty in thinking abstract terms (Nicholl, 1986).

In teaching genetic engineering, students often fail to grasp the concepts because they are not sure about the forms of the molecules involved. A simple approach to this problem is to provide materials from which the students can make models of various things (Nicholl, 1986). The level of sophistication an be varied from basic models up to detailed construction in which the relative sizes of components and the base sequence in certain areas are important. Thus, as the student's awareness grows, more detail can be included in the model making/teaching situation.

The models construction approach can be used to demonstrate the principle of genetic engineering to a wide range of ages and abilities. In addition, the models could substitute for practical exercise in an area where practical work is difficult and not available.

B. Computer-assisted Learning Approaches

Computer-assisted learning (CAL) programmes can be a useful aid to teach the basic principles of genetic engineering (Dewhurst et. al., 1989). They provide an alternative to conventional teaching methods and students generally take readily to this form of teaching. The programme makes extensive use of colour, graphics, and animation which all contribute to improved presentation of materials and enhance learning experience. One advantage of CAL software is that assessments can be incorporated into the programmes which allow the student and the teacher to measure how much of the presented information has been understood. Dewhurst et. al. (1989) have described a CAL programme which presents an investigative approach that makes students learn by discovery. Briefly, the student is led into an imaginary laboratory and must choose from shelves those essential items (e.g. re-agents, starting materials, techniques) to progress through several stages culminating in the production of genetically engineered bacteria. An assessment of how much of the factual information the student has learned is provided in the form of a computer "game" which is not only challenging but also fun to play.

C. Multimedia or Hypermedia

During the past several decades, the virtual perfection of several audiovisual technologies including television, video, computer, and random-access laser disks has come of age. Taken alone, none has lived up to its potential as a teaching tool. However, multimedia programmes now offer the potential to link these technologies into a flexible system that allows individuals to structure their own learning experiences. Using multimedia learning programmes, students can actively explore a complex information field that access multiple analog and digital sources (including video, photographs, art work, sound, and text) according to their preferences of information use. It is expected that multimedia programmes would play a useful role in teaching of biotechnology.

D. Research-based Teaching Approach

Biotechnology is stimulating and, in combination with research, offers the students the opportunity to acquire practical skills through practical experience and the analysis of set experiments. Original research projects generate a considerable amount of enthusiasm among the participating young adults and there can be little doubt that they provide a better learning method than reworking tried experiments. In addition, original research projects offer the students the opportunity to perform work which is interesting, often exciting and (above all) has a purpose (Seenath, 1988a). Furthermore, they teach students scientific methods and the uncertainty of research and "unteach" the attitude that there is a predetermined right and wrong answer to any given problem. Finally, research unleashes the intellectual capacity of a child's mind from the boundaries set by a teacher and in doing so, overcomes the low boredom thresholds of many children (Burton, 1987).

There are a number of problems faced by teachers who would wish to introduce practical work on biotechnology to their course as the technology is new, expensive, and there are health and safety limitation (Miller, 1993). Different strategies have been implemented to circumvent these problems. (Harrison et.al. 1992) have made available a kit based on research equipment for loan to schools on a rota basis. Sponsorship and loan of equipment and reagents from supply companies, and school students visit research establishments where they carry out supervised practical work are certainly strategies which many teachers find a necessity (Miller, 1993).

4. Conclusion

Successful biotechnology education in schools requires high quality curriculum materials, knowledgeable and effective teachers, and a supportive learning environment in the classroom, the school, the home, and the community.

Society can benefit considerably by the early introduction of biotechnology course work and original research projects into schools. Even if some high school students do not choose careers in biotechnology, an educated public is essential for a modern society. Technological literacy is mandatory for the development of : good managers and bankers who can understand the constraints of developing biotechnology products; government policy-maker who will be sensitive to both opportunity and danger; legal advisers who will act judiciously; and journalists who can discuss the issues of the day Lucidty (Seenath, 1983b).

REFERENCES

Boone, C.K. (1984). Moral fantasy in genetic engineering. *American Biology Teacher.* **46**, 449-456.

Bud, R. (1993a). The uses of life : A history of biotechnology Cambridge Univ. Press, Cambridge, UK.

Bud, R. (1993b). 100 years of biotechnology : Events and publications that modulated the industry's place in society. *Bio/Technology.* **11**, 514-515.

Burton, P.B. (1987). Biotechnology in high school : Research for tomorrow. *Trends in Biotechnology.* **5**, 293-294.

Dewhurst, D.G., Meehan, A.S., Williams, A. and Woods, D. (1989). A CAL programme to teach the basic principles of genetic engineering—a change from the traditional approach. *Journal Biological Education.* **23**, 218-222.

Disone, L. (1988). Teaching recombinant DNA technology in high school biology courses. *American Biology Teacher.* **50**, 368-374.

Fiksel, J. and Covello, V.T. (Eds.) (1986). *Biotechnology risk assessment : Issues and methods for environmental introductions.* Pergamon Press, New York.

Fox, M.W. (Ed.) (1992). *Superpigs and Wondercorn : The brave new world of biotechnology.* Lyons & Burford, New York.

Glass, B. (1993). Models for curriculum reform : The new generation of BSCS programmes. *Innovative Science Education.* March 1.

Hardin, G. (1968). The tragedy of the commons. *Science.* **162**, 1244–1245.

Havrison, J., Sampson, J. and Harrison, J.(1992). Enhancing understanding of recombinant DNA technology. *Journal of Biological Educational.* **26**, 1–11.

Hassler, S. (1994). Biotech's role in science education. *Bio/Technology.* **12**, 647.

Ingram, D.S. (1992). Towards an informed public. *Proc. Royal Society, Edinburg.* **99B**, 121-134.

Johnson, R.B. (1993). Biotechnology and the public interest. *Bio/ Technology.* **11**, 180.

Michlos, D.A., Bloom, M.V. and Kruper, J.A. (1989). *Re-tooling biology education for the gene age.* DNA Learning Centre, Cold Spring Harbor Laboratory, New York.

Micklos, D.A. (1990). DNA science and education. *Carolina Tips.* **53**, 41-43.

Micklos, D.A. (1992). *Genetic testing : An educational imperative to our schools.* DNA Learning Centre, Cold Spring Harbor Laboratory, New York.

Miller, M.B. (1993). DNA technology in schools : a straightforward approach. *Biotechnology Education.* **4**, 15-21.

Myers, R. (1985). Recombinant DNA technology in the high school biology laboratory. *American Biology Teacher.* **50**, 43–45.

Nicholl, D.S. (1986). The use of simple models in the teaching of genetic engineering. *Journal of Biological Education.* 2, 12–13.

Olsen, S. (1986). *Biotechnology : An industry comes of age.* Washington D.C., National Academy Press.

Seenath, L. (1988a). Biotechnology in schools. *Bio/Technology.* **6**, 105.

Seenath, L. (1988b). Expanding the horizones. *Bio/Technology Education.* 6, 108-110.

Thomas, R.G. (1988). Recombinant DNA made easy : 1. "Jumping genes". *American Biology Teacher.* **50**, 101-106.

II. PLANT GENETIC ENGINEERING FOR UNDER-GRADUATES

Recent advances in the techniques and application of plant genetic engineering have created unprecedented opportunities for the genetic manipulation of plants (Brill and Barton, 1983). The ability to alter a cell's genetic make-up through the sophisticated technology of genetic engineering is having an enormous impact on plant science. Plant genetic engineering technology can telescope years of labourious plant breeding into a few hours of genetic manipulation, offering the prospect of massive increases in food and crop production at a time when human populations are still rising steadily, and when global food stocks have rarely looked more precarious. Further, the entrance of this technology into the market place has brought about revolutionary and exciting applications that have the potential for great economic impact (Sawahel, 1994).

It does appear, however, that plant genetic engineering teaching programme, especially at under-graduate level, have not advanced as plant genetic engineering research has done. The problems underlying this education morass are vast (Micklos, 1990). Plant genetic engineering education must be a real priority. From undergraduate students come the future scientists who may discover new strategies for crop improvement (Campbell, 1989).

This chapter, therefore, describes the development and nature of a coherent, systematic programme in plant genetic engineering at undergraduate level. This programme would ideally equip students to undertake a career in this field and ensure that they have achieved an adequate and comprehensive training in all aspects of the field. This, in turn, would enable them to gain positions in research and industry.

Target (Gaining Entry to the Programme)

The students should have a biological science background, e.g. introductory courses n Botany, Agriculture, Genetics, Molecular biology or any other related subjects, i.e. Senior level students.

1. *Plant Genetic Engineering Programme*

The potential impact of plant genetic engineering techniologies on the genetic improvement, and crop plants has generated considerable interest, enthusiasm, and optimism in the scientific community and is in part responsible for the rapidly expanding biotechnology industry.

The anticipated role of plant biotechnology is based on elegant demonstrations in model experiments systems that new hybrids, mutants, and genetically engineered plants can be obtained, and the resumption that the same procedures can be adapted successfully for important crop plants.

Knowledge of the structure, function, and regulation of plant genes is scare, and basic research in this area is still limited. On the other hand, a considerable body of knowledge has accumulated on the isolation and culture of plants from tissue cultures of many plant species, isolated mutant cell lines, obtained somatic hybrids by protoplast fusion, regenerated genetically engineered plants from single transformed ells, and achieve large-scale rapid clonal propagation of plants (Sawahel, 1994).

A. Objectives

Plant genetic engineering is now widely used in a variety of basic research programmes as well as in biotechnology industry. Unfortunately, no comprehensive under-graduate teaching programme-describing the numerous techniques and their uses—is available (Wymer, 1989). This programme, therefore, focuses entirely on the basic laboratory procedures and their applications, including plant cell and tissue culture technology, plant genetic resources, plant molecular biology, plant genetic manipulations, and research projects.

B. Class Format

Candidates would study compulsory modules as indicted in Fig. 2.1 This full-time, four semesters programme is of two academic years duration (Table 2.1).

The class format includes lectures, discussion, students presentation, and an open laboratory.

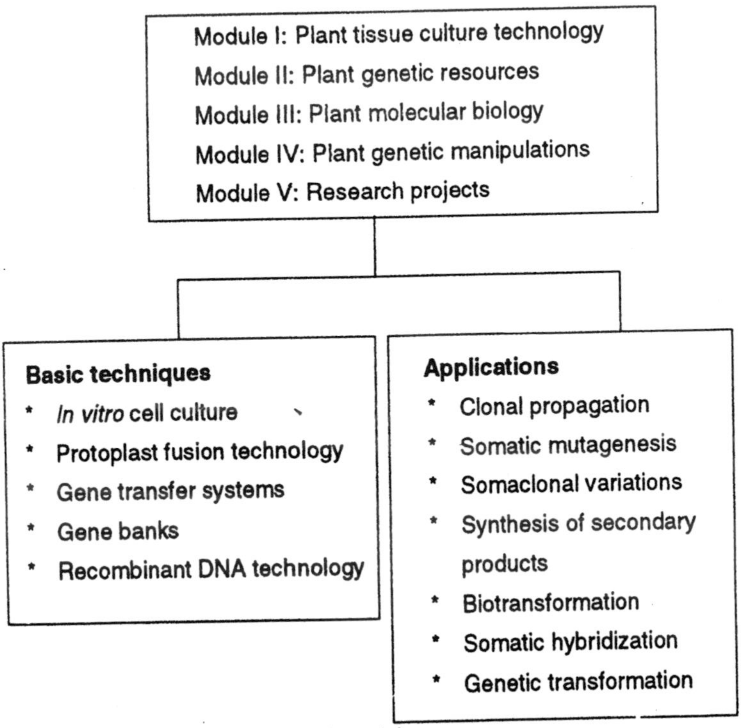

Fig. 2.1. Schematic representation of the programme.

Table 2.1 : Programme Time-table

Academic year	*Semester*	*Period*	*Module*
The first	1	Oct.-Dec.	Plant tissue culture technology
		January	Plant genetic resources
	2	Feb.-April	Plant molecular biology
		May	Examination
The second	1	Oct.-Jan.	Plant genetic manipulations
	2	Feb.-April	Research projects
		May	Examination

Module I : Plant Tissue Culture Technology

A. Basic Techniques

The term "plant tissue culture" is commonly used to describe the *in vitro* and aseptic cultivation of any plant part on a nutrient medium. The techniques of plant cell and tissue cultures have a long history of innovation and evolution. Yet, ironically, the underlying concept of the technique is simple and remains essentially unchanged since the time it was first outlined by Heberlandt in 1902.

This sub-course focuses on the following :

* Organization of plant tissue culture laboratory.
* *In vitro* cell, tissue and organ cultures.
* Transfer of plantlets to soil.

B. Applications

Within the past ten years, the art of plant cell culture has reached a point where it can be considered applicable to economic problems. The advantages of cell culture over the conventional agricultural production of plant material are numerous. The production of botanical products would be possible independent of environmental factors, such as climate, plant pests, and seasons and it would be possible to produce them at any place on the earth. The quality of the raw products could reach a uniformly never observed with field grown material. The production of important drugs like morphine could be done under state control to prevent abuse (Riazuddin, 1988). The length trials of agricultural propagation and cultivation could be shortened.

Finally, the ever expanding world population will have a drastically increased demand for supplies, thus occupying agricultural areas which otherwise could be used for food production.

This sub-course focuses on the following :

* Clonal propagation.
* Somatic mutagenesis.
* Somaclonal variations.
* Synthesis of secondary products.
* Bio-transformation.

Module II : Plant Genetic Resources

Germplasm resources, or more broadly speaking plant genetic resources (PGR), are the basic material for crop improvement. Genes have been repeatedly transferred from non-adapted cultivars and landraces to adapted types by classical plant breeding methods. Genetic resources of cultivated plants and their wild relatives have been found to be genetically diverse. Genetic diversity may be expressed as gross differences among cultivars in morphology and physiological processes due to allelic differences at many loci or at a single locus. The key to successes in plant breeding and research has been the ready access to PGR.

A. Gene Banks

Gene banks have arrived on the centre stage of scientific and public-policy debates. Intense public interest in genetic engineering has raised expectations that biotechnology will unveil dramatic improvements in crop plants. While breakthroughs in genetic engineering are occurring with increasing speed, options for the future are being foreclosed by the erosion of one of the world's most important heritages, the genetic diversity of our crop plants and their wild relatives.

Gene banks can be either *ex situ,* where seeds or plant parts are preserved outside their areas of growth, or *in situ,* where plants including wild relatives of crops, are maintained in natural preserves. Gene banks contain plants preserved in seed from or in outside plots, known as field gene banks.

Module III : Plant Molecular Biology

In the past decade, the power and scope of genetic engineering and biotechnology have become apparent (Sawahel and Fukui, 1995). Recombinant DNA technology permits the isolation and amplification of individual genes, the study of their structure and function, their transfer to various species, and expression of their products (Dewhurst et al., 1989).

A. Recombinant DNA Technology

Genetic engineering derives from and depends on the manipulation of bacterial genetics (parson, 1988; Sawahel et. al. 1983) using an increasing number of specialized enzymes (restriction endonucleases) as re-agents and small circular DNA plasmides as vectors (Micklos, 1987; Watson et. al., 1983).

This sub-course focuses on the following :

* Growth of *E. coli* and spectrophotometer calibration.
* Growth of *Bacteriophage lambda* and purification of lambda DNA.
* Isolations, purification, and characterization of plasmid DNA.
* Sub-cloning of phage genes into plasmid DNA.
* Transformation of *E. coli* with recombinant DNA.
* Biological analysis of recombinant plasmids.
* Size analysis of recombinant plasmids.
* Isolation of plant DNA.
* DNA restriction and analysis by Southern hybridization.

B. Plant Genetics

This sub-course focuses on the structure and expression of plant genomes (nuclear, mitochondrial, chloroplast) (Sawahel, 1996).

Module IV : Plant Genetic Manipulations

Plant genetic manipulation is the molecular genetical strategy of transferring genetic material from plant to plant (Sawahel and Cove, 1922b).

This course focuses on the basic technology of plant genetic manipulations as well as its applications.

A. Basic Techniques

* Organization of genetic manipulations laboratory.
* Protoplast fusion technology.
* Gene transfer systems.

B. Applications

* The production of hybrid plants.
* The production of transgenic plants.

Module V : Research Projects

Projects provide an opportunity for students to work on a plant genetic engineering problem at greater depth than what they learn in the limited time during class practical. However, plant genetic engineering projects are extremely difficult to design and assess in a fair and uniform manner because of the great diversity of areas that can be lumped under the umbrella of plant genetic engineering (Sawahel and Cove, 1992a). It may, therefore, be impractical to have each individual student to do a high quality, advanced project. The group project can be an alternative to the individual project (Lui, 1993). The group project has a number of advantages : the project scope can be enlarged and the concept of team-work an be introduced.

Because the student's eventual employment may not be in the same area as their project, it is important that students be trained in basic principles and concepts that would be useful to them no matter what area of plant genetic engineering they eventually branch into.

According to Lui (1993), the following points should be learnt by the students :

* How to draft an action plan at the start of the project?
* How to set realistic and reachable objectives?
* How to plan and design experiments?
* How to manage the time properly?
* How to do a literature search?
* How to use statistical tools, and to analyse and interpret results?

* How to write a valid scientific report?
* How do defend ones work in the interview and/or oral examination.

2. Assessment

The assessment system should ensure that student have a good practical and numerical ability as well as an excellent grasp of the theories (Lock & Dunkerton, 1989; Mehler, 1992). In addition, other desirable qualities of a good biotechnologist should be assessed (Hodgson, 1987; Hassler, 1993).

There are a variety of procedures which can be used for assessment such as :

* A formal examination at the end of each academic year.
* Oral presentation for the research project.
* Practical reports based on experiments performed and/or a practical examination.

REFERENCES

Brill, W.J. and Barton, K.A. (1983). Prospects in plant genetic engineering. *Science.* **219**, 671-675.

Campbell, P.N. (1989). Manpower and training needs for biotechnology. *Biotechnology and Applied Biochemistry.* **11**, 525-526.

Dewhrst, D., Meehan, A.S., Williams, A. and Woods, D. (1989). A CAL Programme to teach the basic principles of genetic engineering—a change from the traditional approach. *Journal of Biological Education.* **23**, 218-222.

Hassler, S. 91993). Biotech's role in science education. *Bio. Technology* **12**, 647.

Hodgson, C.P. (1987). Social and legal issues of biotechnology : An education perspective. *Ohio Journal of Science.* **87**, 148-153.

Lick, R. and Dunkerton, J. (1989). Evaluation of an inservice course on biotechnology. *Research in Science and Technological Education.* **7**, 171-181.

Lui, J. (1993). Designing and assessing undergraduate biotechnology projects. *Biotechnology Education.* **4**, 37–39.

Mehler, A. (1992). Integration of examination and education. *Journal of Biochemistry Education.* **20**, 10-14.

Micklos, D. and Freyer, G. (1987). *DNA Science : A first laboratory course in recombinant DNA Techniques.* Cold Spring Harbor Laboratory, N.Y.

Micklos, D.A. (1990). DNA Science and education. *Carolina Tips.* **53**, 41–43.

Nicholl, D.S. (1986). The use of simple models in teaching of genetic engineering. *Journal of Biological Education.* **20**, 12-13.

Parson, K.A. (1988). Recombinant DNA technology : A topics course for undergraduates. *Journal of Biochemistry Education.* **65**, 325-326.

Riazuddin, S. (1988). Development of training programmes in biotechnology safety and risk assessment. *Bio Essays.* **9**, 131-134.

Sawahel, W. and Cove, D. (1992a). Model systems for studying plant molecular biology. *Biotechnology Education.* **3**, 167-172.

Sawahel, W. and Cove, d. (1992b). Gene transfer strategies in plants. *Biotechnology Advances.* **10**, 393-412.

Sawahel, W., Sastry, G., Knight, C. and Cove, D. (1993). Development of an electro-transformation system for *E. coli* DHIOB, *Biotechnology Techniques.* **7**, 261-267.

Sawahel, W. (1994). Transgenic plants : performance, release and containment. *World Journal Microbiology and Biotechnology* **10**, 139-144.

Sawahel, W.A. (1996). A proposed postgraduate programme in plant genetic engineering. *Biotechnology Education.* **7**, 1-7.

Sawahel, W. and Fuki, K. (1995). Gene cloning in plants : Innovative approaches. *Bio/Techniques.* **19**, 106-114.

Sawahel, W. (1996). Plant molecular and cellular laser microsurgery. *World Journal of Microbiology and Biotechnology.* 12:561–566.

Watson, J.D., Tooze, T. and Kuvtz, D.T. (1983). Recombinant DNA. *A Short Course.* Scientific American Books.

Warner, P.E. (1989). Biotechnology education. *Ag. Biotech. News and Information.* **1**, 687-690.

III. PLANT GENETIC ENGINEERING FOR POST-GRADUATES

In the early 1980's, there was intense discussion on the exact nature and definition of plant biotechnology (Kennedy, 1991) and the best ways of teaching it (O'Kennedy, 1991). There is still considerable disagreement as to whether or not plant biotechnology should be taught at the undergraduate level. It does appear, however, that many organizations and universities now recognize the utility and teaching potential of an undergraduate degree in biotechnology (Peretti & Cherry, 1989). Furthermore, there is a need for a flexible advanced programme especially in the fast moving field of plant genetic engineering, to ensure that post-graduates are kept up to date and achieve an adequate and comprehensive training in all aspects of the field.

This chapter describes the development and nature of such a post-graduate programme in plant genetic engineering. This programme would ideally equip students to undertake a career in this field and ensure that they are highly skilled which would enabled them to gain positions in research and industry.

The Target (Gaining Entry to the Programme)

The students should have a biological sciences background, e.g., B.Sc. in Botany, Agriculture, Molecular Biology, Genetics or any other related subjects.

1. Plant Genetic Engineering Programme

Within the past few years, the production of genetically modified plants has become common place, and their value in fundamental and applied studies has been described in numerous reports (Fig. 3.1). However, before such plants are accepted as having a commercial value, the stability and expression of the introduced gene (s) must be confirmed over several generations and preferably within a range of different genetic backgrounds. Moreover, such studies need to be conducted under field conditions and the agronomic performance of the material confirmed in relevant trials.

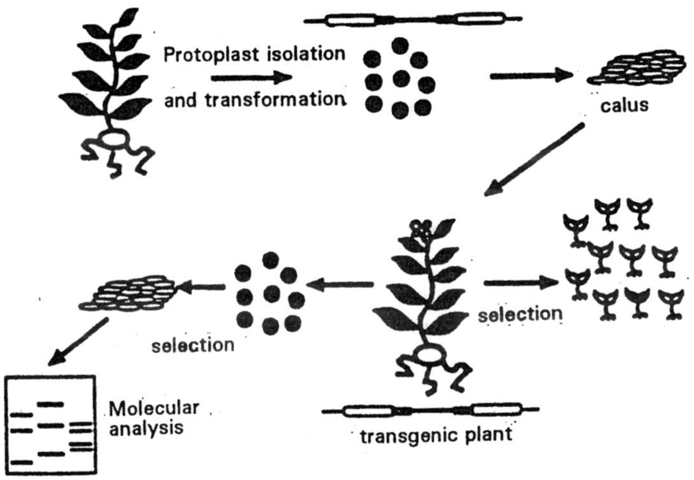

Fig. 3.1: The Production of Genetically Modified Plants

A. Objectives

This programme focuses on the production of genetically modified plants (Fig. 3.2), from the initial stages of the genetic modification process in the laboratory (including searching for the desirable gene from the gene pool, gene isolation and gene transfer) to their release stage in the field. Candidates would study compulsory modules as indicated in Fig. 3.3. Each module consists of lectures, together with the acquisition of practical skills. This full-time, three semester programme is of 12 months duration (Table 3.1).

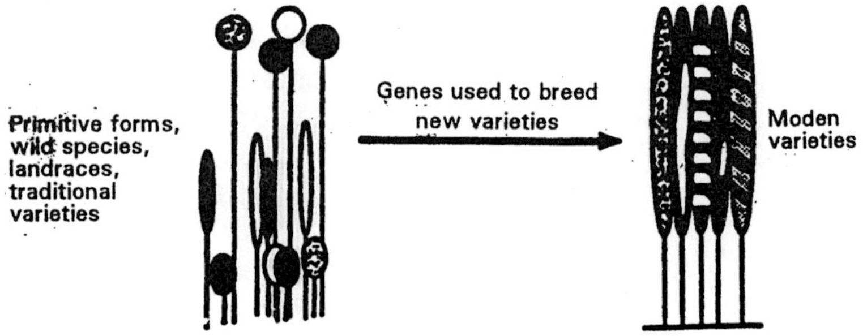

Fig. 3.2: Plant Genetic Engineering

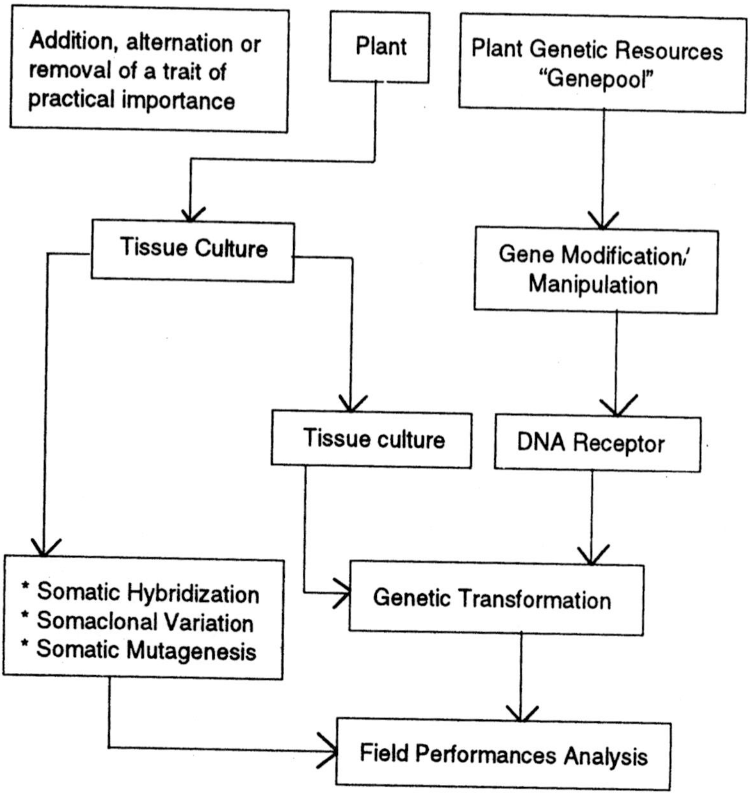

Fig. 3.3: Schematic representation of plant genetic engineering programme

Table 3.1 : Programme Time-table

Semester	*Period*	*Module*
1	October	Plant Genetic Resources
	November	Plant Genetic Resources
	December	Plant Tissue Culture
	January	Plant Tissue Culture
2	February	Study and Research Skills
		(a) Literature Survey and Research Projects
		(b) Presentation Skills
	March	Gene Modification/Manipulation
	April	Gene Modification/Manipulation
	May	Genetic Transformation
	June	Genetic Transformation
3	July	Field Performance Analysis
	August	Field Performance Analysis
	September	Study and Research Skills
		(b) Grant application
		(c) Writing a research paper
		(d) Research patenting
	October	Examination

Module I : Plant Genetic Resources

Plant genetic resources hold the key to food security and sustainable agricultural development. The world's growing populations, which depend on fixed areas of farmland, will need to produce new, higher yielding, disease resistant and environmentally suitable plant varieties, i.e. plant genetic resources 'genepools' are the building blocks for plant improvement.

The module concentrates on the following :

A. Genetic Diversity

Biological diversity encompasses the total variability of lifeforms existing on this planet. Plant genetic resources, a subset of biodiversity, contain genetic material which is the source of the vast variety of plant life on Earth.

Contents

The course outlines the variability of life forms in terms of plant species, populations and ecosystems.

B. Genetic Resources and Biotechnology

Biotechnology has already made significant contributions to work on genetic resources. Tissue culture techniques and molecular methods have been rapidly deployed in key areas.

Contents

This course focuses on the following technologies for the conservation of plant genetic resources :

* *Ex situ* conservation.
* *In situ* conservation.
* DNA storage
* Disease Indexing
* Identifying useful genes
* Evolution and species relationship

Module II : Plant Tissue Culture

A. Protoplast Culture & Fusion Technology

Until now, a few genes for economically important characteristics have been isolated. In most cases, these characters are coded for by families of interacting genes, multiple genes or polygenes. These genes can either occur scattered throughout the genome or clustered within blocks on the arms of the chromosome.

Current gene transfer strategies can successfully transfer single genes. For example, the Ti-plasmid of *Agrobacterium tumefaciens* has been used to transfer 14 Kb of DNA. However, a single polygenic trait could contain up to 20 individual genes comprising 500 Kb of DNA. Most plasmids could not contain all the DNA encoding a single polygenic characteristic.

Protoplast fusion offers the unique possibility of combining unrelated nuclear and cytoplasmic genomes thereby producing hybrid cells and, ultimately, hybrid plants. The maintenance of two unrelated genomes in a hybrid is not always desired since this condition has been associated with morphological and cytogenetic abnormalities often resulting in partial or complete sterility. To produce viable and fertile hybrids, researchers have irradiated protoplasts from one parental line (the donor) in order to pulverize the chromosomes and facilitate the elimination of substantial amounts of the donor genome. In this manner, a specific trait that is native to the irradiated donor genome may eventually be transferred into the genome of the recipient. As this is accomplished without the conservation of the entire donor genome, the term *asymmetric somatic hybridization* has been applied to such hybridization studies. The effectiveness of asymmetric somatic hybridization as a method for introducing a novel trait into a regenerate is dependent upon the gene or genes which are being transferred, and on the ability to select hybrids *in vitro.* This method has potential use for the transfer of molecularly uncharacterized traits and multigenetic traits.

B. Somaclonal Variation

Somaclonal variation is genetic variation generated during tissue culture and is viewed as an option for obtaining genetic variation. Somaclonal variation offers an opportunity to uncover natural variability and to use this variability for the development of new varieties. Variation has been observed in over 30 species of agronomic and ornamental plants regenerated from *in vitro* culture. The high frequency of leaf and flower morphology and colour variants in regenerated plants was used to develop "Velvet Rose".

Many of genetic changes that have been detected either in spontaneously generated mutants or as a result of induced mutations are also detected *via* somaclonal variation. In addition several unique genetic phenomena arise at higher than expected frequencies or occur only as a consequence of somaclonal variation such as cytoplasmic gene changes, chromosome rearrangements, mitotic crossing over, gene expression, changes in the copy number of repeated DNA sequences, activation of transposable elements and tissue specific changes. One obvious strategy for the use of somaclonal variation is to introduce the best available varieties into a cell culture and to select among regenerated plants, or their progeny for incremental improvement over existing varieties while adding one additional trait, such as disease resistance or herbicide resistance.

This course focuses on the genetic basis, and current and future applications of somaclonal variation.

C. Somatic Mutagenesis

This course focuses on the combination of somaclonal variation and somatic mutagenesis.

Module III: Gene Modification/Manipulation

It is now possible to transform most of the important plant species. However, the application of this technology to rational plant-improvement is currently limited by a shortage of cloned genes for important traits.

This module concentrates on the following:

A. Gene Isolation/Manipulation

All techniques for gene isolation exploit one or more of the four characteristics that define genes: they have a defined primary structure (sequence); occupy a particular location within the genome; encode RNA with particular expression patterns; and, most genes have a function.

Contents

This course focuses on recent technological advances in plant-gene isolation and identification. The following approaches to gene cloning in plants are studied.

* Gene-product based cloning.
* Insertional inactivation.
* Subtractive methods.
* Map-based cloning.
* Large-scale sequencing..
* Cloning by complementation.
* Shotgun rescue.
* Chromosome micro-dissection.

B. Alteration or Removal of a Trait of Practical Importance

Cloned plant genes are generally used to examine some aspects of genetic mechanisms, to examine the role of the gene product in the life of the organism or to add, alter or remove a trait of practical importance. The approaches by which these objectives are realized include:

* Antisense or co-suppression.
* Gene inactivation.
* Altered expression of cloned genes.

Module IV : Genetic Transformation

In recent years, the term transformation has been extended to include the uptake of any DNA molecules by any type of cell, regardless of whether the uptake results in a detectable change in the cell or whether the cell involved is bacterial, fungal, animal or plant. As a result of the genetic revolution, gene transfer systems have been developed for many plant species, and routine transformation of certain plants now takes place in laboratories all over the world.

Recombinant DNA technology is an important tool for genetic manipulation. The application of this technology is dependent on the availability of efficient systems for the transfer of foreign genetic material into cells capable of giving rise of fertile plants. In other words, the key step in the genetic engineer's technology is the ability to transfer genes into plants. Genetic transformation offer a plethora of ways to explore gene function and regulation and is a potential means of modifying plants for crop improvement.

This Module concentrates on the following:

A. Gene Delivery Systems

This course focuses on the recent progress which has been made in the field of gene transfer systems in plants. It includes the following systems:

Natural transformation systems

* *Agrobacterium spp.*

Direct gene transfer

* Electroporation.
* Electroinjection
* Electrophoresis.
* Macroinjection.
* Microinjection.
* Liposome system.
* Polycation-mediated transfer.
* Ca-DNA co-precipitation.
* UV laser microbeam.
* Particle bombardment.
* Silicon carbide fiber-vortex.
* Sonication.

B. Organelle Transformation

Transformation of plastid genomes has several potential problems that nuclear transformation does not share. For one thing, it may be more difficult for DNA to cross the plastid double membrane than the nuclear membrane. In addition, plastid genomes are present in much higher copies than nuclear genomes — the single *Chlamydomonas* chloroplast has 80 genome copies and higher plants can have 100 or more plastids, each with many genome copies. Therefore, for a transformed genome to replace all copies of the original genome strong selection pressure for prototropic growth or for antibiotic resistance must be applied.

This course focuses on plastid transformation systems and their use in addressing fundamental questions of plastid biology including mechanisms of plastid gene regulation, regulatory interactions of plastid nuclear genes, editing and translation of mRNA and photosynthesis.

C. Genetic Recombination

Presently, one of the most useful parameters for distinguishing different modes of recombination remains the base sequence homology or lack of it, between the two DNA's which react to form a recombinant molecules. This is partly due to the lingering obscurity of the DNA sequence and the number of enzymatic functions involved in genetic recombination.

This course focuses on the types and possible molecular mechanisms of both intra and extra-chromosomal recombination.

D. Gene Targeting

The ability to target introduced DNA sequences to homologous sites in the genome provides a powerful tool for molecular genetic analysis.

This course focuses on approaches for gene targeting such as retransformation, restriction enzyme-mediated events and factors which might play a role in gene targeting such as gene dosage (copy number) and integration sites (position effect).

Module V: Field Performance Analysis

A major goal of plant genetic engineering is the production of transgenic crops expressing novel genes encoding agronomically desirable traits. A number of transgenic plants expressing a number of different genes which confer enhanced resistance to insect pests and herbicides, have been produced. If this technology is to be effective in the field, it is essential that the benefits of the introduced characters are not outweighted by any yield penalties.

This module concentrates on the following three main topics:

A. Inter-transformation Variability

Uniform and continuous expression of the transgene is of considerable importance for the application of gene transfer systems, especially if transgenic plants are to be used in applied plant breeding programmes.

Plant transformants produced *via Agrobacterium* transformation or direct gene transfer vary widely in the expression of the transgene. The level of protein coded for by an alien gene varies 10 to 50-fold among individual transformants within the same experiment and substantial inter-transformant variability also occurs in the amount of gene transcript. In addition, unexpected expression of the marker gene has been reported.

Contents

This course focuses on the causes of inter-transformant variability such as the copy number of the transgene, gene dosage; the integration site of the transgene (position effect), truncation, rearrangement or repetition of the transgene; experimental and biological factors or a defined genetic variability; epigenet effects; the effect of the environment; mutation; the loss of the gene by recombination events; integration of the transgene into genes essential for gamete or embryonic development; and suppression of gene expression.

B. Marker Genes

Despite the scientific advances made in crop improvement, the commercialization of genetically modified plants has been slowed down by public concerns about the impact of these plants on the environment and human health. These concerns centre on problems that might arise as more land is planted with genetically modified plants.

Many scientists are concerned that useful genes are introduced into plants in combination with so-called marker genes; genes that usually encode antibiotic or herbicide resistance. Therefore, there is fear that herbicide-resistant genes might somehow be picked up by weeds, pathogenic bacteria might acquire the antibiotic resistant genes and, the introduced foreign trait might change the normal physio-logy of a modified organism or generate unpredicted phenotype changes which might result in a new, aggressive creature.

Contents

This course concentrates on the classes of the marker genes, its advantages and issues about their safety.

C. Gene Flow

It has been suggested that the primary risk in releasing genetically modified crops is the natural transfer of the modified genes to wild relatives *via* cross pollination. Gene flow has considerable potential as an evolutionary force. Some theories indicate that even a moderate rate of gene flow is sufficient to counteract the diversifying effects of local or directional selection or genetic drift. Gene flow has been of little interest to plant ecologists and evolutionary biologists. This is because most of the traits which are introduced by traditional breeding methods (such as dwarfing) are maladaptive in wild relatives and thus have little ecological impact. However, many of the improvements targeted by biotechnology including resistance to pests, herbicides, diseases and stress (e.g. cold, drought and salinity), will be equally beneficial to wild relatives.

Contents

This course concentrates on the gene flow and strategies for the isolation of transgenic plants genetically.

Module VI : Study and Research Skills

This module concentrates on the following:

A. Literature Survey and Research Projects

The projects are selected from the five main areas of the programme. The Literature Survey is associated with the background area of the research project. Reports on both are combined as a thesis and form a major part of the assessment. The Literature Survey and the research project allow the students to gain a high level of practical expertise "hands-on" experience and to extend their knowledge of a particular area in detail.

B. Presentation Skills

The emphasis should be on the following:

* The practical skills need for effective presentation including understanding the audience, planning the presentation, platform presence, coping, with nerves and answering questions. Practice with supportive feedback should be key features. This will increase the student's impact when giving lectures formal, presentations or keynote speeches.

C. Grant Application

The emphasis should be on the following:

* Getting grant funding including opportunities and methods; overview of the main sources of funding; finding, researching and approaching the funder.
* Writing the proposal including guidelines for writing the proposal and a practical exercise on proposal writing.

D. Writing a Research Report

The emphasis should be on the following:

* Writing a research paper including getting started, writer's block and organisation.
* Placing the paper including choosing a journal, submission, rejection, rewriting and acceptance.
* The view of the publisher, editor, referee and printer.

E. Research Patenting

The patenting of the whole organisms or parts of their genetic information is one of the most contentious areas of biotechnology.

The emphasis should be on the following:

* An introduction to patents and procedures.
* Intellectual property.

2. Assessment

The assessment system should ensure that students have a good practical and numerical ability as well as an excellent grasp of the theories. There are a variety of procedures which can be used for assessment such as:

(1) A formal examination at the end of the programme.

(2) Oral presentation for the research project.

(3) Practical reports based on experiments performed and/or practical examination.

REFERENCES

Aronsfeld, E. (1992). *Essential Presentation Skills,* Staff Development, University of Leeds, UK.

Avison, D. (1989). *The Project Report: A Guide for Students,* Peter Francis, Dereham.

Basic Facts: Patents, The Patent Office, UK.

Buzan, T. (1987). *Use Your Head,* BBC Publication, London.

Cove, D., Sawahel. W., Knight, C. and Wallace, J.(1994)., Genetic Transformation of the Moss *Physcomitrella Patens, J. Experimental Botany.* **45S**, 7.

Debouck, D.G.(1992) Views on Variability in *Phaseolus* beans. *Annu. Rep. Bean Improvement Coop.* **35**, 9-10.

ESRC (1991). *Postgraduate Training Guideline,* Economic and Social Research Council, Swindon.

Gowers, E. (1973). *The Complete Plain Words,* HMSO, London (Now in Penguin).

Harrison, N. (1987). *Successful Writing.* Peter Francis, Dereham.

Hill, P.J. (1988). *Study Skills,* Pan Book, London.

Hills, P.J. (1993). *Writing Proposal for Grant Funding. Staff Development,* University of Leeds, UK.

How to prepare a UK patent application. The Patent Office, UK.

Howard, K. and Sharp, P.A. (1983). *The Management of a Student Research Project* , Gower, Aldershot

Jain, H.K. (1988). Plant genetic resources and policy. *Trends in Biotechnol* **6**,73-77.

Kennedy. M.J. (1991). The evolution of the word "Biotechnology". *Trends in Biotechnology,* **9**, 218-220.

Knight, C., Sawahel, W. and Cove, D. (1993). Gene flux in the moss Physcomitrella patens- the fate of foreign DNA in three classes of transformants *J.Experimental Botany.* **44**, 32.

Knupffer, H. and Perry, M.C. (1992). An international barley documentation system: concepts and strategies In: *Barley Genetic Resources.* pp. 20-26. International Crop Network Series No. 9. IBPGR, Rome.

Leytham, G. (1990). *Managing Creativity,* Peter Francis, Dereham.

Medawar, P. (1981). *Advice to a Young Scientist.* Pan Books, London.

O'Connor, M. and Woodford, F. (1978). *Writing Scientific Papers in English,* Pitman Medical, Tunbridge Wells.

O'Kennedy, R. (1991). Development of an undergraduate degree programme in Biotechnology. *Biotechnol. Ed.,* **2**, 27-30.

Paroda, R.S. and Arora, R.K. (1992). Genetic resources, crop improvement and sustainable agriculture. In: *Biodiversity—Implication for Global Food Security.* Swaminathan, M.S. and Jana, S. (Eds.) pp. 59-78. Macmillan (India) New Delhi, India.

Patent Protection, The Patent Office, UK.

Patents— A Source of Technical Information. Patent Office, Department of Trade, UK.

Peretti, S. and Cherry, R.(1989). The need for and of biochemical engineers *Biotechnol,* **7**, 1124.

Perry, M.C. (1992), IBPGR and the biodiversity network—Interest and scope of involvement. In: *Needs and Specifications for a Biodiversity Network,* Canhos, V., Lange, d., Kirsop, B. E., Nadi, S. & Ross (Eds.) Proc. Int. Workshop, Campinas, Brazil. pp. 50-52 UNEP, Campinas, Brazil.

Sawahel, W. and Cove, D. (1992). Gene Transfer Strategies in Plants, *Biotechnol. Advances,* **10**, 393-412.

Sawahel, W. and Cove, D. (1992). Model systems for studying plant molecular biology. *Biotechnol. Ed.,* **3**, 167-172.

Sawahel, W., Onde, S., Knight, C. and Cove, D. (1992). Transfer of foreign DNA into *Physcomittrella Patens* Protonemal tissue using the gene gun. *Plant Mol Biol. Rep.* **10**, 315-316.

Sawahel, E., Sastry, G., Knight, C. and Cove, d. (1993). Development of an electro-transformation system for *E. colf* DHIOB. *Biotechnol. Techniques.* **7**, 261-266.

Sawahel, W., (1993). Gene transfer strategies. *Rice Biotechnol. Quarterly* **14**, 35-37.

Sawahel, W., Knight, C. and Cove, D. (1993). Transformation of the moss *Physcomitrella patens* by microprojectile bombardment. *J.Experimental Botany.* **44S**, 45.

Sawahel, W., (1994). Transgenic Plants: Performance, Release and Containment. *World J.Microbiology & Biotechnol,* **10**, 139-144.

Sawahel, W. (1994). Transgenic Plant Technology. *Rice Biotechnol. Quarterly.*

Sawahel, W., Knight, C, Wallace, J. and Cove, D. (1994). Co-and retransformation of the moss *Physcomitrella Patens. J. Experimental Botany,* **45S**, 23.

·Sawahel, W. and Ali, A. (1994). Callus induction and maintenance of *Zea mays* Kernels. *Biotechnol. Letters,* **16**, 397-400.

Sawahel, W., Knight, C. and Cove, D. (1994). *Characterisation of the Classes of Transformants of the Moss Physcomitrella Patens.* The Genetical Society spring meeting. "Chromosome stability, Genome projects and genetic regulation." University of Wales, Swansea, 28-31 March.

Sawahel, W. and Fukui, K. (1994). Gene cloning in plants: Innovative approaches.

Stibic, V. (1982). *Tools of the Mind,* North Holland, Amsterdam

Wallace, J., Knight, C. and Sawahel, W. (1994). Maintenance of non–selected transforming DNA in unstable transformations of the moss *Physcomitrella Patens. Plant Science.* Submitted

What is Intellectual Property. The Patent Office, UK.

Withers, L.A., (1992). *In vitro* conservation. In: *Biotechnology of Perennial Fruit Crops.* pp. 169-199. Hammerschlag, F. & Litz, R.E. (Eds.) CABI, UK.

Withers, L.A. (1992). *New Technologies for the Conservation of Plant Genetic Resources.* First Int. Crop Science Congress, Ames, Iowa, 14-22 July 1992.

FURTHER READINGS

Adams, R. and Admas, J. (1992). *Conservation of Plant Genes: DNA banking and in vitro biotechnology*. Academic Press, U.K.

Bains, W. (1993). *Biotechnology: From A to Z*. Oxford University Press, U.K.

Bajaj, Y.P. (1986). *Biotechnology in Agriculture and Forestry*. Springer-Verlag Berlin-Heidelberg, Germany.

Brown, C., Campbell, I and Priest, F. (1987). *Introduction to Biotechnology*. ELBS/Blackwell Scientific Publications, U.K.

Bruening, G., Harada, J., Kosuge, T. and Hollaender A. (1985). *Tailoring Genes for Crop Improvement: An Agriculture Perspective*. Plenum Press, U.K.

Burrell, M. (1993). *Enzymes of Molecular Biology*. Humana Press, U.S.A.

Crabbe, M. (1990). *Enzyme Biotechnology*. ELLIS Horwood, U.K.

Crierson, D. (1990). *Plant Genetic Engineering*. Chapman and Hall, New York, U.S.A.

De Robertis, E.D. and De Robertis, E.M. (1995). Cell and *Molecular Biology*. Waverly International, India.

Dixon, R. (1985). *Plant Cell Culture*, IRL Press, Oxford.

Gardner, E., Simmons, M. and Snustad, D. (1984). *Principles of Genetics*. John Wiley and Sons, Inc., U.K.

Gatehouse, A., Hilder, V. and Boulter, D. (1992). *Plant Genetic Manipulation for Crop Protection*. CAB International, U.K.

Giller, K.E. and Wilson, K.J. (1991). *Nitrogen Fixation in Tropical Cropping Systems*. CAB International, U.K.

Glick, B. and Pasternak, J. (1994). *Molecular Biotechnology*. ASM Press, Washington, D.C.

Glover, D. and Hames, B. (1995). *DNA Cloning*. IRL Press, Oxford.

Gresshoff, P. (1992). *Plant Biotechnology and Development*. CRC Press. London.

Grierson, D. (1991). *Developmental Regulation of Plant Gene Express*. Chapman and Hall, New York, U.S.A.

Gupta, P. and Tsuchiya, T. (1991). *Chromosome Engineering in Plants. Genetics, Breeding, Evolution*. Elsevier Science Publishers, Netherland.

Gurr, S., McPherson, M. and Bowles D. 91992). *Molecular Plant Pathology*. IRL Press, Oxford.

Gustafson, P. (1990). *Gene Manipulation in Plant Improvement*. Plenum Press, U.K.

Hames, B. and Glover, D. (1990). *Gene Rearrangement*. IRL Press, U.K.

Hames, B. and Higgins, S. (1995). *Gene Probes*. IRL Press Oxford.

Herrmann, R. and Larkins, B. (1990). *Plant Molecular Biology*. Plenum Press London.

Kelly, T. and Stillman, B. (1988). *Enkaryotic DNA Replication*. Cold Spring Harbor Laboratory, U.S.A.

Key, J. and Mclntosh, L. (1987). *Plant Gene Systems and their Biology*. Alan Liss Press, New York, U.S.A.

Kucherlapat, R. and Smith, G. (1988). *Genetic Recombination*, American Society for Microbiology, U.S.A.

Lai, E. and Birren, B. (1990). *Electrophoresis of Large DNA Molecules*. Cold Spring Harbor Laboratory Press, U.S.A.

Lal, R. and Lal, S. (1993). *Genetic Engineering of Plants for crop improvement*. CRC Press, London.

Lodish, H., Baltimore, D., Berk, A., Zipursky, S., Matsudaria, P. and Darnell, J. (1995). *Molecular Cell Biology*. W.H. Freeman and Company, New York, U.S.A.

Morrison, I. (1992). *Advances in Plant Cell Biochemistry and Biotechnology*. JAI Press, U.K.

Murray, D. (1991). Advanced Methods *in Plant Breeding and Biotechnology*. CAB International, U.K.

Old, R. and Primorse, S. (1994). *Principles of Gene Manipulation*. Blackwell Scientific Publication, U.K.

Persley, G.J. (1990) *Agricultural Biotechnology: Opportunities for International Development*. CAB International,. U.K.

Polak, J. and McGee, J. (1990). In *situ Hybridization Principles* and *Practice*. Oxford University Press, U.K.

Sharp, W. Evans, D., Ammirato, P. and Yamada, Y. (1984). *Handbook of Plant Cell Culture*. Collier MacMillan Publishers, London.

Shaw, C. (1988). *Plant Molecular Biology*, IRL Press, Oxford.

Synder, L., Freigelder, D. and Hartl, D. (1985). *General Genetics.* Junes and Bartlett Publishers, Boston.

Thottappilly, G., Monti, L.M. Raj, D.R. and Moore, A.W. (1992). *Biotechnology: Enhancing Research on Tropical Crops in Africa.* International Institute of Tropical Agriculture (IITA)/ Technical Centre for Agricultural and Rural Cooperation (CTA), IITA, Ibadan, Nigeria.

Walden, R. (1989). *Genetic Transformation in Plants.* Prentice-Hall Press, U.S.A.

APPENDIX

For the aspiring student of plant genetic engineering and biotechnology, there are a number of universities around the world to go to for undergraduate or postgraduate degrees (B.Sc., M.Sc., Ph.D.). The following are some of them :

Australia

* School of Biological and Environmental Sciences, Murdoch University, Perth, Western Australia 6150.
* Department of Botany, University of Melbourne, Parkville, Victoria 3052.
* Research School of Biological Sciences, The Australian National University, P.O. Box 475, Canberra City, ACT 2601.
* Centre for Molecular Biotechnology, Queensland University of Technology, 2 George Street, Brisbane Qld 4001.

Austria

* Institute for Genetics and Microbiology, University of Vienna, Dr. Bohrgasse, A-1030, Vienna.
* Institute for Botanik der Universitat Wien, Abteilung Cytologic and Genetik, Rennweg 14, A-1030 Vienna.

Canada

* Plant Biotechnology Institute, University of Saskatchewan, 110 Gymnasium Road, Saskatoon, Saskatchewan, 57N OWO.
* Department of Biology, Concordia University, 1455

de Maisonnenve Blud West, Montreal, Quebec H3E IM8.

* Crop Science Department, University Guelph, Guelph, Onatario, N1E 2W1.
* Biology Department, Carleton University, Ottawa.
* Centre of Forest Biology, Department of Biology, University of Victoria, P.O. Box 1700, Victoria, B.C. V8W 2Y2.
* Department of Biology, University of Waterloo, Waterloo, ON N2L 3E1.
* Department of Biological Sciences, University of Calgary, Calgary, Alta., TZN 1N4.

Denmark

* Department of Plant Biology, Royal Veterinary and Agricultural University, Thorvaldsensuej 40, 1871 Frederiksberg C, Copenhagen.

Finland

* Institute of Biotechnology, P.O. Box 45, Karvaamokuja 3A, FIN-00014, University of Helsinki.

France

* Centre de Physiologic Vegetate, UA CNRS 1457, Universite Paul Sabatier, 118, Route de Narbonne, 31062 Toulouse Cedex.
* Laboratoire de Physiologic Vegetale, Fuculte des Sciences, Universite de Bretagne Occidentale, 29275 Brest Cedex.
* Laboratoire de Biochimic, Analytique et Synthese

Bioorgansque, Bat 303, Universite Lyon 1, 69622 Villeurbanne, Cedex.

Germany

* Department of Biology, Humboldt University Berlin, Berlin D-10115.
* Institut for Genetik, Technische Universitat Braunschweig, Spielmannstrasse 7, D-38023, Braunchweig.
* Institut of Plant Physiology (260), University of Hohenheim, P.O. Box 700562, D-7000 Stuttgart 70.
* Max-Planck-Institute for Zuchtungsforschung, Abterlung Genetische Grundlagen der Pflanzenzuchtung, Egelspfad, D-5000 Koln 30.
* Institut for Genetik, Universtat Zu Koln, D-5000 Koln 41.
* Institut for Angewandte Genetik, Freie Universitat Berlin, Albrecht-Thaer-Weg 6, 1000 Berlin 33.
* Institute for Pflanzenphysiologic, Freie Universitat Berlin, Konigin-Luise-Strasse 12–16, D-14195 Berlin.
* Institute for Genetik (W6), Universitat Bielefeld, D-33501 Bielefeld.
* Botanisches Institut, Spielmannstrasse 7, 38106 Braunschweig.
* Lehrstuhl for Pflanzenokulugic and Systematik, Universitat Bayrenth, Postfach 10 12 51, D-8580 Bayrenth.
* Botanisches Institut der Ludwig-Maximilians, Universitat, Menzinger Str. 67, D-8000 Munchen.
* Biologisches Institut II der Universitat Freiburg, Schanzlestrasse 1, D-7800 Freinrg.
* Gesellschaft for Strahler and Umweltforschung, Institut for Biochemische Pflarzenpathologic, Ingolstadter Landstrasse 1, D-8042 Neuherbag.

* Institut for Allgemeine Botanik, Universitat Hamburg, Ohnhorststr 18, D-2000 Hamburg 52.
* Institut for Botanik and Botanischer Garten, Westf Wilhellms Universitat, Scholo Bgarten 3, D-48149 Munster.
* Technical University Hamburg-Harburg, Biotechnology/Technical Microbiology, Denickestrabe 15, D-21071 Hamburg.
* Institute for Phytomedizin, Universtat Hohenheim, D-7000, Stuttgart 70.

Japan

* Department of Biology, Okayama University, Okayama 700.
* School of Agricultural Science, Nagoya University, Nagoya 464-01.
* Department of Agricultural Chemistry, Faculty of Agriculture, The University of Tokyo, Bunkyo-Ku, Tokyo 113.
* Department of Botany, Faculty of Science, Hokkaido Universite, Sapporo 060.
* Nagasaki University, Bunkyo-machi 1-14, Nagasaki 852.
* Laboratory of Vegetable and Ornamental Horticulture, Faculty of Agriculture, Shimane University, Nishikawatsu-Cho 1060, Matsue 690.
* Department of Biology, Nagoya University, Furo-Cho, Chikusa-Ku, Nagoya 464.
* Department of Biotechnology Science, Faculty of Biology-Oriented Science Technology, Kinki University, 930 Nishimitani, Uchita, Naga, Wakayama, 649-64.

Netherland

* Department of Experimental Botany, University of Nijmegen, Toernooiveld 1, NL-6525 ED Nijmegen.
* Department of Biochemistry, Gorlaens Laboratories, Leiden Univ., Einsteinweg 5, 2333 CC Leiden.
* Department of Plant Physiology, Agricultural Univ., Arboretumlaan 4, 6703 BD Wageninger.
* Department of Molecular Biology, Wageninger Agricultural University, Dreijenlaan 3, 6703 HA, Wageninger.
* Department of Genetics, University of Groninger, Karklaan 30, NL-9751 NN Haren.
* Department of Molecular Cell Biology, University of Utrecht, Padualaan 8, 3584 CH Utrecht.

Sweden

* Department of Molecular Genetics, Uppsala Genetic Center, Swedish University of Agricultural Sciences, P.O. Box 7010, S-75007 Uppsala.

Switzerland

* Swiss Federal Institute of Technology, Institute of Plant Sciences, ETH-Zentrum, Universtatstrasse 2, CH-8092 Zurich.
* Lehrstuhi for Biochemic and Pflanzen, Ruhr-Universitat Bochum, Universitatsstra 150, 44801.

United Kingdom

* Department of Applied Biology, The University of Hull, Hull HU6 7RX.

* University of Manchester, Manchester M13 9PL.

* Department of Genetics and Microbiology, Institute of Food Research, Norwich Research Park, Colney, Norwich, NR4 7UA.

* Department of Applied Biology and Biotechnology, Scraptaft Campus, De Montfort University, Leicester LE7 9SU.

* Department of Botany, University of Leicester, University Road, Leicester LE1 7RH.

* Department of Biological Sciences, University of Durham, South Road, Durham DH1 3LE.

* Department of Physiological and Environmental Science, School of Agriculture, University of Nottingham, Sutton Bonington, Longhborough LE12 5RD.

* Department of Biochemistry, University of Cambridge, Tennis Court Road, Cambridge CB2 1QW.

* Wolfson Institute of Biotechnology, The University of Sheffield, Sheffield S10 2TN.

* Biology Department, University of Essex, Wivenhoe Park, Colchester CO4 3SQ.

* Department of Botany, School of Biological Sciences, University Park, Nottingham, NG7 2RD.

* Leicester Biocentre, University of Leicester, Leicester LE1 7RH.

* Department of Biological Sciences, University of Exeter, Washington Singer Laboratories, Perry Road, Exeter, EX4 4QG.

* School of Biological Sciences, University of Leeds, Leeds, LS2 9JT.

* Division of Biosciences, University of Hertfordshire, Hatfield Campus, College Lane, Hatfield Herts, AL10 9AB.

United States of America

* Department of Botany, The University of Texas, Austin, TX 78713.
* Department of Biology, Yale University, P.O. Box 6666, New Haven, CT 06511.
* Department of Biochemistry, University of Arizona, Tucson, AZ 85721, U.S.A.
* Department of Biological Sciences, State University of New York, Buffalo, NY 14260.
* Plant Molecular Genetics Department, 269 Ellington Plant Sciences Building, University of Tennessee, Knoxville, TN 37901-1071.
* Department of Botany, Arizona State University, Tempe, AZ 85287-1601.
* Ohio State Biotechnology Centre, Ohio State University, 206 Carmack Road, Columbus, OH 43210.
* Laboratory of Plant Cell and Molecular Biology, 1253, Fifield Hall, University of Florida, Gainesville, FL 32611.
* Centre for Biotechnology, University of Nebraska-Lincoln, 101 Manter Hall, P.O. Box 880139.
* Department of Biochemistry and Molecular Biology, University of Georgia, Athens, GA 30602-7229.
* Department of Plant Science, The State University of New Jersey, Rutgers, Foran Hall, Dudley Road, Cook College, P.O. Box 231, New Brmswick, JN 08903-0231.
* Department of Biology, University of Virginia, Charlottesville, UA 22903.
* Department of Plant Pathology and Crop Physiology, College of Agriculture, Louisiana State, University Baton Ronge, LA 70803-1720.

* Department of Biological Sciences, Purdue University, West Lafayette, IN 47907.

* Plant Gene Expression Centre, University of California at Berkeley, 800 Buchanan Street, Albany, CA 94710.

* Department of Horticulture, Centre for Gene Research and Biotechnology, Oregon State University, Corvallis, OR 97331-7304.

* Department of Horitculture, Biotechnology Institute, Pennsylvania State University, University Park, PA 16802.

* Texas A&M University, Agricultural Experiment Station, 2415 East Highway 83, Weslaco, TX 78596.

* Biology Department, Washington University, Saint Louis, MO 63130-4899.

* Department of Biological Sciences, Louisiana State University, Shreseport, LA 71115.

* Louisiana State University, Agricultural Centre, Red River Research Station, Bossier City, LA 71113.

* Laboratory of Plant Molecular Biology, The Rockefeller University, 1230 York Avenue, New York, NY 10021-6399.

* Department of Agronomy, University of Illinois, 1201 West Gegory, Urbana, IL 61801.

* United State Department of Agriculture, University of Wisconsin, 1630 Linden Drie, Madison W1 53706.

* Department of Agronomy, University of Kentucky, Lexington, KY 40456.

* Department of Molecular Genetics and Cell Biology, University of Chicago, Chicago, IL 60637.

* Division of Plant and Social Sciences, College of Agriculture and Forestry, West Virginia University, Morganton, WV 26505-6108.

* Centre for Molecular Genetics, University of California, San Diego La Jolla, CA 92093-0116.

* Department of Agronomy, North Dakota State University, Fargo, ND 58105.